To Aixa, who brings so much joy to our family, and special thanks to Asa and Dorian for your support and love.

- Mekael -

Dedicated to Dot, Paw Paw, and Grandpa Chuck

copyright @ 2021 by Mekael C. Black
edited by: Nancy Haight

All rights reserved. No part of this book may be used or reproduced in any number whatsoever without written permission of the author, except in the case of quotations embodied in articles and reviews.

This is a work of fiction. Names, characters, places and incidents are either products of the author's imagination, or are used fictitiously.
Any resemblance to actual persons, living or dead, or historical events is entirely coincidental.

BY: MEKAEL C. BLACK

ILLUSTRATED BY: YENUSHKA DUNUWILA

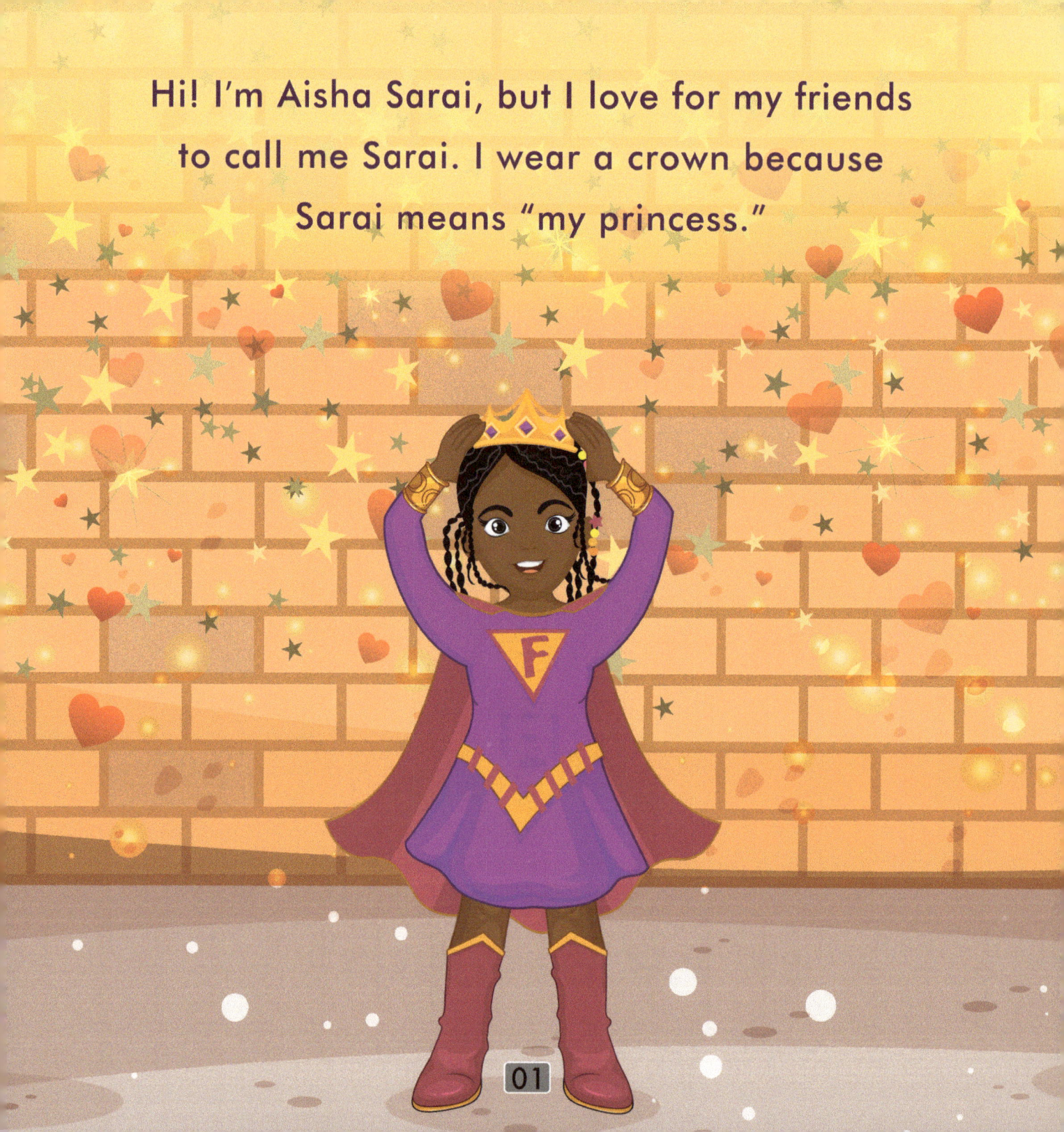

Hi! I'm Aisha Sarai, but I love for my friends to call me Sarai. I wear a crown because Sarai means "my princess."

When I wake up in the middle of the night,
and it's dark, I will not be in fright.

I am not alone. God lives in me, and my angels are working day and night.

It's the first day of school. New teacher and new students-what will I do?

I will not be scared. I will be cool because God whispered in my ear, "I am with you."

Oh golly, I have to give a speech in front of the WHOLE class!

No jitters here, because God did not give me a spirit of fear!

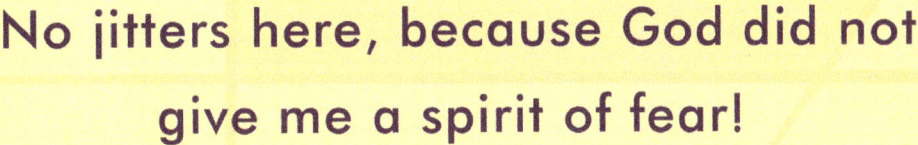

My parents bought me a new bike.
It's pretty, but it's tall!
I don't want to fall.
My brother told me not to think like that at all.

He said, "You can do it!" He was right! I can do it! I will do it!

I'm doinggggggggggg it!

I can do all things through Christ who strengthens me.

A kid was really mean to me at school. I told my teacher. I told my parents, and we said a prayer, "Sarai is strong and courageous. She will not be afraid of a mean kid, for the Lord goes with Sarai!" My big brother also told me, "You may be small physically, but you're big spiritually!"

Guess what? The next day, the kid apologized to me. Now, we play together at recess.

The weatherman said a BIG storm was coming.
At first, I got scared.

My dad read a story where Jesus calmed the storm. Jesus told the storm, "Peace! Be still," and it was still! I looked out the window, pointed my hand to the sky, and shouted, "Peace! Be still!" I felt so brave, and I was no longer afraid.

It was the day of my first piano recital. I was supposed to be excited, but I was having nervous thoughts. "What if I forget the notes? What if the people laugh? What if I fall off my seat?" I looked at my parents, and my parents smiled at me. I could hear their voices saying, "God is with you, Sarai. He gave you a gift to use for His glory. He delights in you!"

I took a deep breath, adjusted my seat, played my song, and I got a standing ovation!

My parents enrolled me in swim lessons.
Why did they do that? I didn't ask for that!
I CAN'T swim!

My mom said, "God has given you strength and courage! You will learn to be a great, fearless swimmer." By the end of the class, I was diving in the pool! Mom was right. I did it!

I was sad and scared when I found out that I had to say goodbye to grandpa. My dad prayed with me, "Sarai, God's peace is with you; do not be worried and afraid. Grandpa is in Heaven, and we will see him again."

I felt so happy after we prayed. God is with me, and my memories of Grandpa are with me forever.

I'm so thankful that God is always with me. I have zero reasons to fear. When fear comes, I will remember the times when I prayed to God. He heard my prayers and answered me. He gave me His peace to overcome all my fears.

PLEASE LEAVE A REVIEW

Please take a moment to rate and review The Fearless Princess on Amazon as this helps others (kids and parents) discover the story. Authors love to hear from their readers!

Thank you and BE FEARLESS!

www.ingramcontent.com/pod-product-compliance
Lightning Source LLC
LaVergne TN
LVHW072011060526
838200LV00010B/326